Design, snip, clip . . .

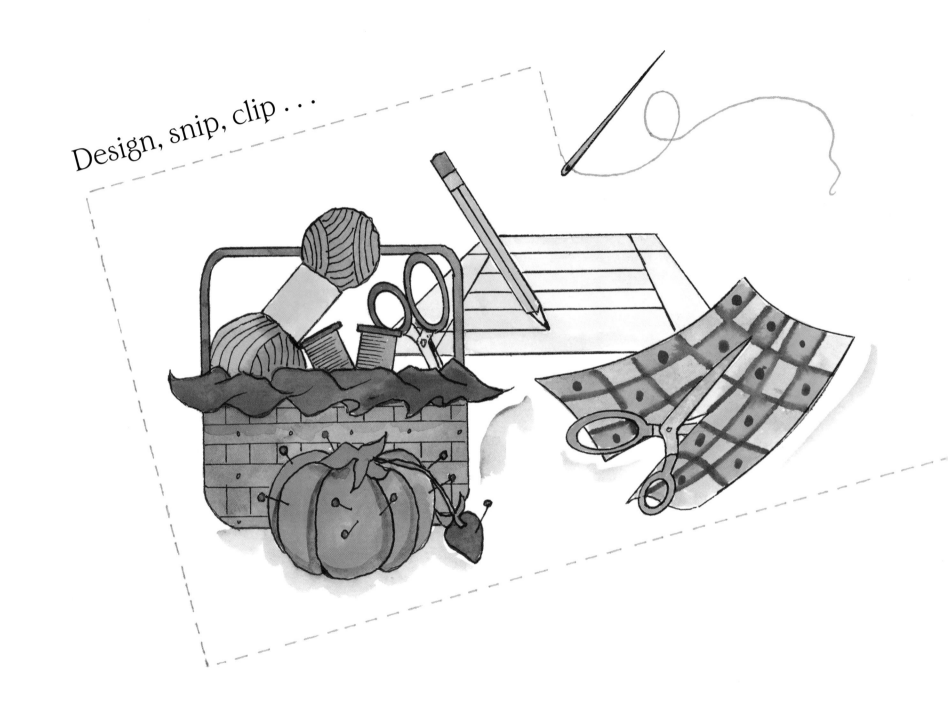

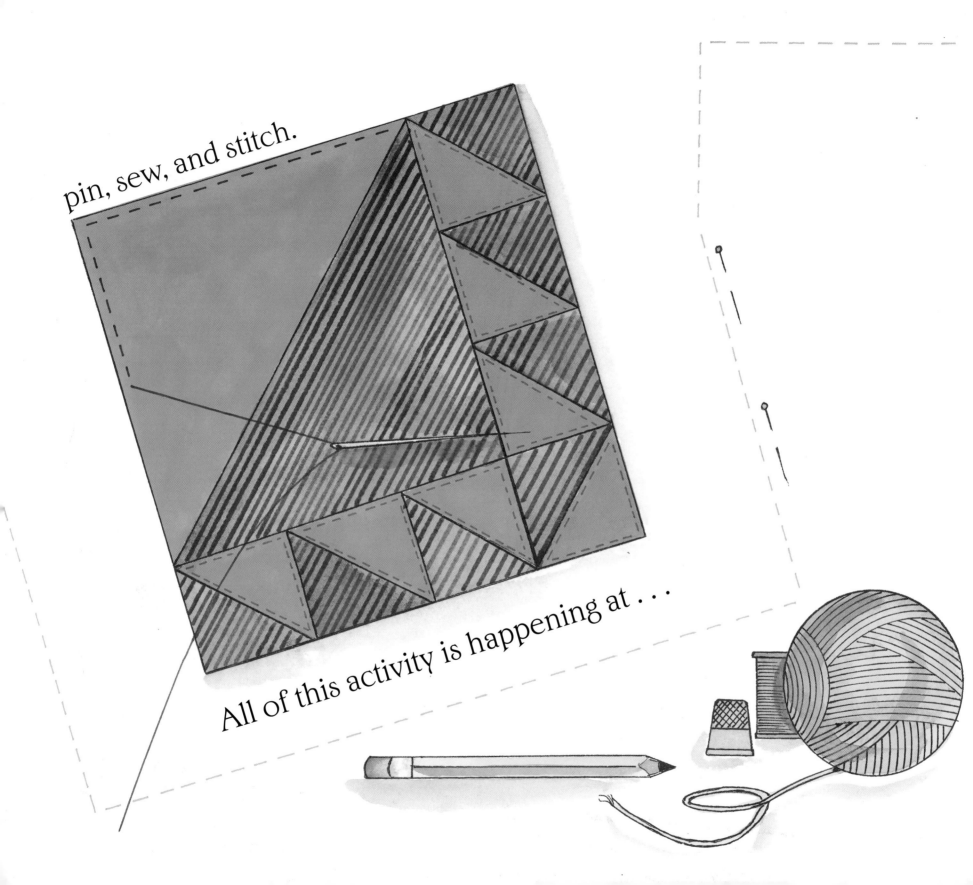

pin, sew, and stitch.

All of this activity is happening at . . .

The Quilting Bee

by Gail Gibbons

HarperCollinsPublishers

Special thanks to
Louise Young of East Corinth, Vermont,
for her expert advice on quilt making.

Also, I want to thank Eula Stevens
for the lovely quilt she made for me.

The Quilting Bee
Copyright © 2004 by Gail Gibbons
Manufactured in China. All rights reserved.
www.harperchildrens.com

Library of Congress Cataloging-in-Publication Data
Gibbons, Gail.
The quilting bee / by Gail Gibbons.
p.   cm.
Summary: An introduction to the process of quilt making, including a history of the
craft, sample quilt patterns, and directions for creating a children's book authors' and
illustrators' quilt.
ISBN 0-688-16397-1 — ISBN 0-688-16398-X (lib. bdg.)
1. Patchwork—United States—Patterns—Juvenile literature.   2. Patchwork quilts—
United States—History—Juvenile literature.   3. Quilting—United States—Societies,
etc.—Juvenile literature.   [1. Patchwork.   2. Quilting.   3. Quilts.   4. Handicraft.]
I. Title.
TT835 .G527   2004   746.46—dc21   2002023310

Typography by Jeanne L. Hogle
2 3 4 5 6 7 8 9 10

First Edition

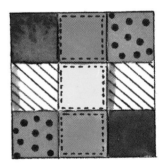

QUILT MAKING REQUIRES ADULT SUPERVISION.

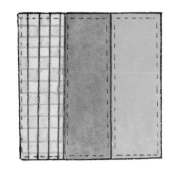

Because bees are good at working together, the word *bee* came to mean people getting together to do some useful work. Have you ever heard of a *spelling bee*?

A group of quilt makers have come together to share their time and many talents piecing together a beautiful quilt. Their group is called a *quilting bee,* or a *quilting circle.*

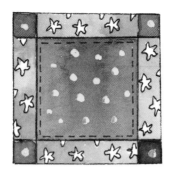

A quilt is a warm bed covering made up of three layers. There's the top layer that usually has a colorful design, the cotton padding in between, and the quilt's backing.

TOP LAYER

PADDING

BACKING

The word *quilt* comes from the Latin word *culcita*, which means "stuffed sack, mattress, or cushion."

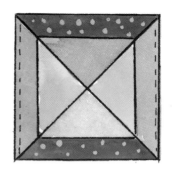

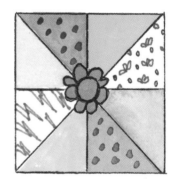

The quilters begin their project by carefully choosing, or designing themselves, a pattern for their quilt. Fabrics of different colors, textures, and patterns soon fill the room.

PINE TREE QUILT BLOCK

The quilters pick and choose the different fabrics they will use. They cut squares, triangles, and other shapes. Then they stitch the shapes together to make patterned squares called *quilt blocks*.

It takes a long time and many gatherings to create all the quilt blocks they will need. Finally the group begins to sew the blocks together. When they are done, they have a beautiful top layer for their quilt.

The top layer, the padding, and the material for the back of the quilt are stretched over a *quilting frame*. The quilters busy themselves stitching and tying the three layers together, using heavy thread or yarn.

QUILTING FRAME

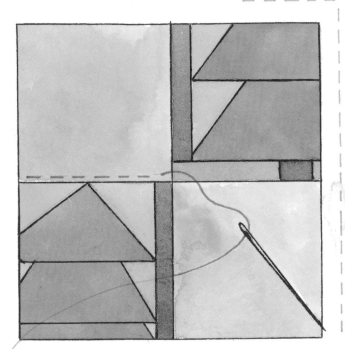

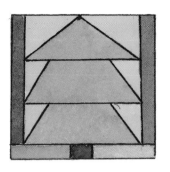

Over time the quilt begins to take shape. The room is full of activity. As the quilters stitch, they talk about the news and what's going on in their town.

The art of quilting goes far back in time. The Egyptians, Chinese, and Turkish people used quilted material in their clothing for warmth. Quilting was also used as a cushion for heavy armor.

FOUR-PATCH block

NINE-PATCH block

The TRIP AROUND THE WORLD pattern was made up of tiny squares of fabric sewn together around one square.

In the United States pioneer women created quilts to keep their families cozy and warm. The simplest quilt blocks were usually the most popular designs for everyday use.

ALBUM QUILT blocks were signed in India ink or embroidery and given as gifts to a special friend or beloved family member.

Sometimes SIGNATURE QUILTS were made to be signed by famous people.

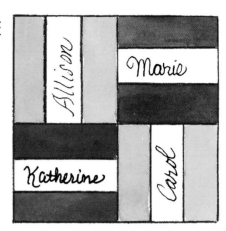

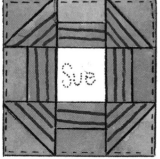

Pioneer families were very proud of their quilts. They created them from precious scraps of cloth. Quilts were made for all sorts of reasons.

The ROAD TO
CALIFORNIA
pattern looks like
a wagon trail.
It is also called the
TRAIL OF THE
COVERED WAGON.

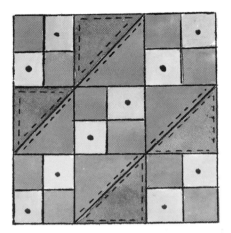

The HILL AND VALLEY
quilt shows the land
the pioneers passed
through along the
journey.

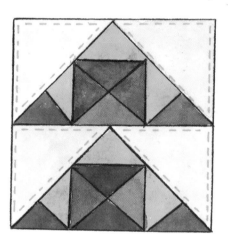

The ROCKY GLEN
quilt shows the rough
trails the pioneers had
to struggle through.

Many quilt patterns had special stories
to tell, such as what pioneers saw and
felt as they traveled west.

BEAR'S PAW

Many quilt patterns represented wild animals.

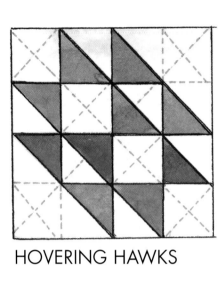

HOVERING HAWKS

On the DOVE IN THE WINDOW quilt, doves seem to be touching their beaks in the center.

What are the creatures in the FISH pattern doing?

The pattern in the WATERWHEEL quilt is a reminder of the millstones used to grind grain.

RAIL FENCE

The LITTLE RED SCHOOLHOUSE design came from the one-room schoolhouses children attended.

LOG CABIN

Pioneer families often made quilts that reminded them of their new homes.

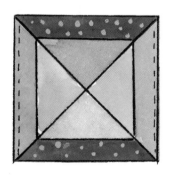

The BABY'S BLOCKS pattern looks like the simple toys that babies played with.

The KITCHEN WOOD BOX quilt reminded early Americans of the wood boxes they stored their firewood in for cooking and warmth.

The FRUIT BASKET quilt celebrated harvesttime.

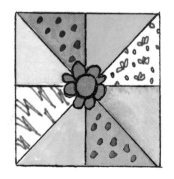

Other quilt designs reflect family life in the settlers' homes.

FLOWERPOT design

WEDDING RING design

The FRIENDSHIP RING quilt got its name because it took a ring of friends to gather the wide variety of fabrics needed to create it. This design is also known as the ASTER or DRESDEN PLATE.

The GRANDMA'S FAN pattern reminded families of their grandmother keeping cool on hot summer days.

Many quilts expressed love and caring for other people.

OCEAN WAVES design

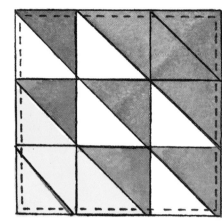

The NORTH WIND pattern looks like the wind moving across the prairie.

Weather played an important role in the everyday life of settlers, as was often seen in their quilt designs.

The WHIRLWIND design shows another kind of weather.

The SUNBURST design says "sunny day"!

CORN AND BEANS quilt

NOONDAY LILY

HOLLYHOCK WREATH

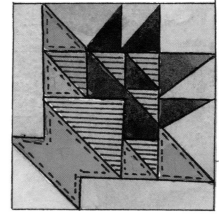

In the GRAPE BASKET
design the purple color
in each basket represents
harvested grapes.

Many traditional
quilt patterns
reflect the foods
planted by the
early Americans.
Others represent
the flowers they
loved to grow.

BEAUTIFUL STAR

EIGHT-POINTED STAR

MILKY WAY

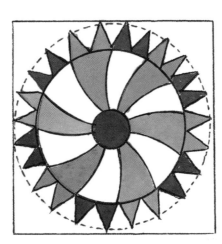

RISING SUN

Many quilt patterns were created from images of the stars of the night sky . . . and, in the morning, the rising sun.

CRAZY QUILT

One traditional pattern is called the *crazy quilt*. These quilts had no special pattern. Instead, many shapes and sizes of fabric were stitched together willy-nilly.

In the past, quilts could only be sewn by hand.

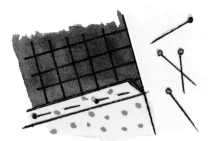

PINS held the fabric together before sewing.

A THIMBLE protected the finger that pushed the NEEDLE through the fabric.

A SCISSORS was used to cut fabric.

A QUILTING FRAME held the quilt's three layers in place while they were stitched together.

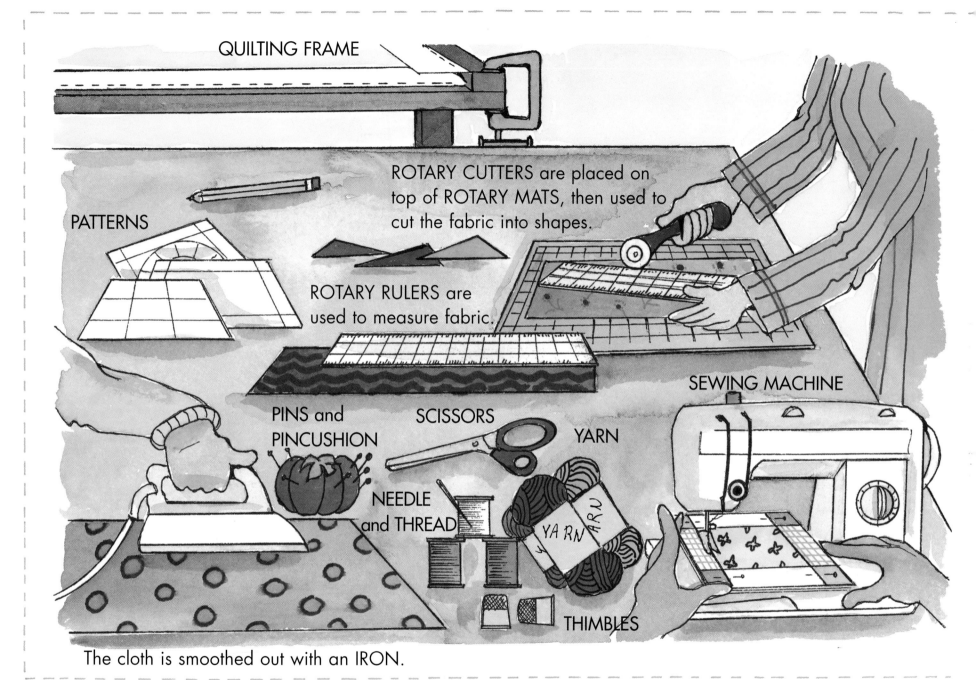

QUILTING FRAME

ROTARY CUTTERS are placed on top of ROTARY MATS, then used to cut the fabric into shapes.

PATTERNS

ROTARY RULERS are used to measure fabric.

SEWING MACHINE

PINS and PINCUSHION

SCISSORS

YARN

NEEDLE and THREAD

YARN

THIMBLES

The cloth is smoothed out with an IRON.

Today, at the quilting bee, the quilt makers use many modern tools to create their quilts and many tools that are familiar.

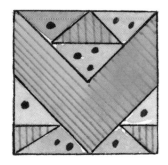

Today there are still county fairs, quilt shows, and contests to choose the most beautiful, original, and interesting quilt. Members of the sewing bee work hard so they can enter their quilt in a local contest.

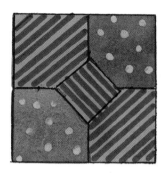

All around the
different stands,
quilts are on
display. Some
have traditional
patterns; others
are not traditional
at all!

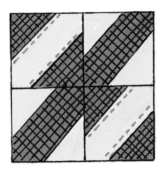

Judges walk by. They take notes, then cluster together to discuss the many quilt designs. The judges want to select a quilt that is truly special.

The judges have made up their minds. They gather in front of the quilting bee and award its entry first place. Quilters agree that the quilt is special because so much good talk, laughter, and friendship were sewn into it. Everyone applauds.

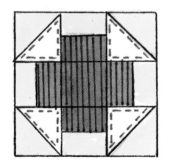

In a few weeks the quilting bee is at it again. . . .

An Authors' and Illustrators' Quilt

These students are planning a quilt project. They choose their favorite authors and illustrators and send each one a square cloth with a letter that describes the quilt project.

Most authors and illustrators are happy to join the project. They sign their names and sometimes make a drawing or a painting on the piece of cloth.

Then they send their quilt squares back to the students.

When all the squares are returned, adults help the students stitch them together into their very own authors' and illustrators' quilt. How special it is!

Design . . . Cut . . . Stitch . . .

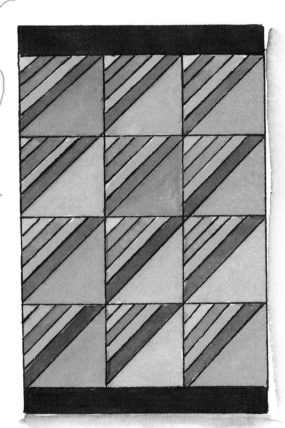

The Amish, a religious group, came to America to create their own farming communities. They are famous for their beautiful traditional quilts.

There are hundreds of traditional quilt designs.

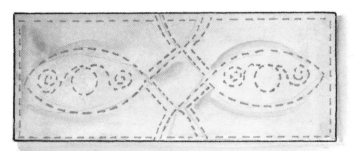

Often quilt makers decorate their quilts by doing fancy stitching on the top.

The TREE OF LIFE is an old colonial pattern. Often it was designed to represent a *family tree.* A family tree shows past and present members of a family.

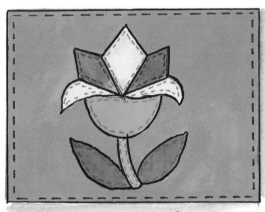

Sometimes APPLIQUÉ is used in quilting. That is when a piece of one fabric is sewn on top of another.

Today quilt makers use their imagination to create designs that are works of art.